First Printing First Edition 2024

adiamondouttherough@gmail.com

ISBN: 979-8-9916047-2-7

Table of Contents

"Diamond Characteristics Activities"

Praise God, fellow Diamonds! Please use this companion journal alongside the A.D.O.R.E. book to express your thoughts on the activities from the book. Be sure to also spend time meditating on the journal's 'Diamond Characteristics' activities." These bonus activities can be found on the following pages:

"The point of a Diamond was chosen by the Lord as the instrument that will cause generations to remember" (Jeremiah 17: 1 NKJV).

_____
_____
_____
_____
_____
_____
_____
_____
_____
_____
_____
_____
_____
_____
_____
_____
_____
_____
_____
_____
_____
_____
_____
_____

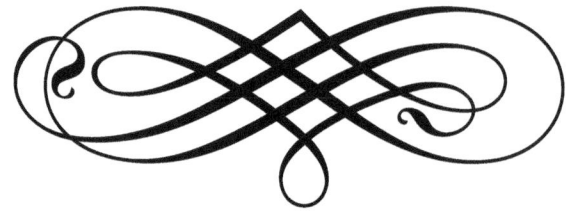

_____

_____

_____

_____

_____

_____

_____

_____

_____

_____

_____

_____

_____

_____

_____

_____

_____

_____

_____

_____

_____

_____

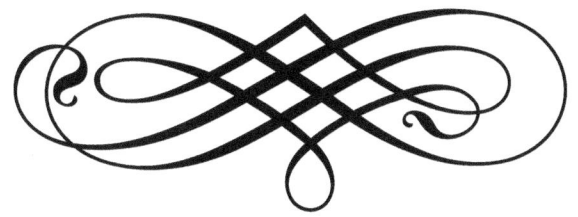

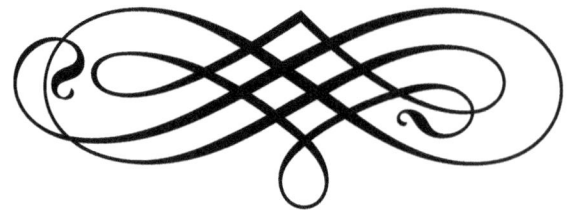

_____

_____

_____

_____

_____

_____

_____

_____

_____

_____

_____

_____

_____

_____

_____

_____

_____

_____

_____

_____

_____

_____

_____

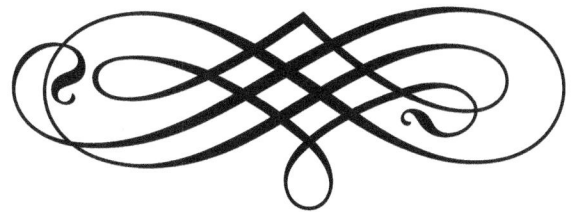

_____

_____

_____

_____

_____

_____

_____

_____

_____

_____

_____

_____

_____

_____

_____

_____

_____

_____

_____

_____

_____

_____

_____

_____

_____

_____

"Diamonds are one of the 12 precious stones used in the second of a total of four rows, all in gold setting instructed to be added to on the breastplate of the Priestly garments" (Exodus 28: 17-21 NKJV).

_____

_____

_____

_____

_____

_____

_____

_____

_____

_____

_____

_____

_____

_____

_____

_____

_____

_____

_____

_____

_____

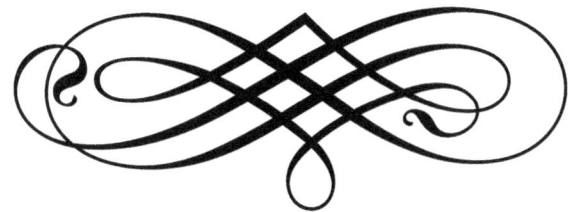

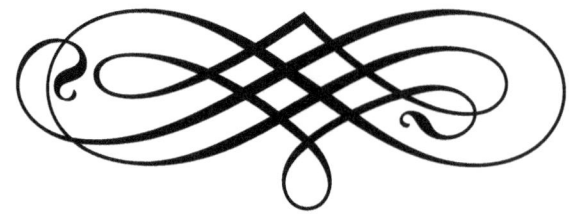

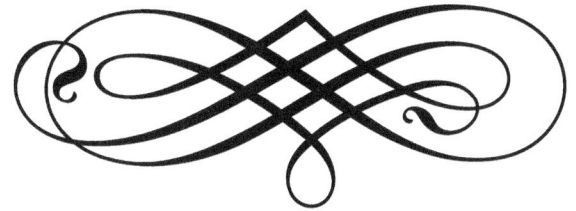

_____

_____

_____

_____

_____

_____

_____

_____

_____

_____

_____

_____

_____

_____

_____

_____

_____

_____

_____

_____

_____

_____

_____

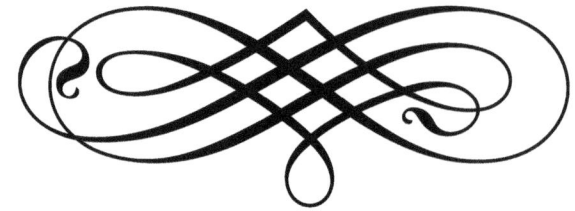

The Strong's Hebrew Concordance 3095 meaning "yalahom" for "Precious Stone"

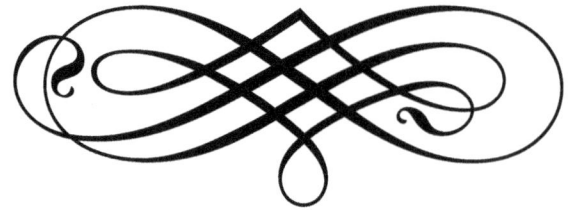

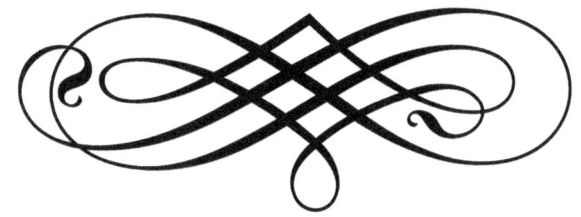

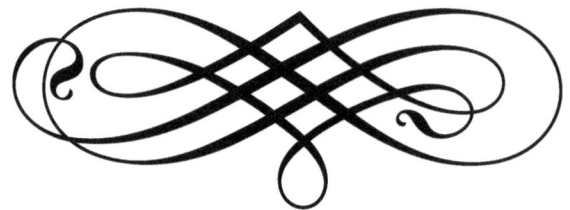

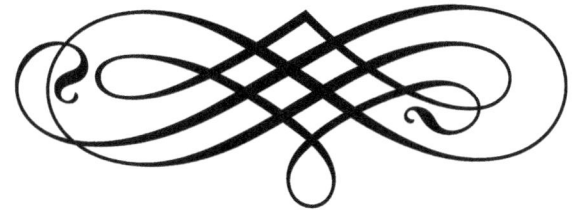

The Strong's Hebrew Concordavnce 8068 meaning "shamir" for " A flint, Adamant or a Thorn. The word adamant is the same root word of diamond.

_____
_____
_____
_____
_____
_____
_____
_____
_____
_____
_____
_____
_____
_____
_____
_____
_____
_____
_____
_____
_____
_____
_____
_____
_____
_____

Resilient

The very essence of a diamond is a symbol of resilience. To be resilient means to have the materials or substance that is required to be able to recoil, to spring or bounce back after being stretched, compressed, or bent. It also means to 'recover' quickly from adverse or difficult conditions. To 'recover well'.

Let's have a Praise Break.

- God made Jonah Resilient to be able to endure 3 days in the stomach of a giant whale.
- God made Joseph Resilient to withstand being:
- uprooted from the only family He known
- conspired on by his own brothers and sold into slavery
- falsely accused of sexual implications,
- imprisoned and He STILL ended up Recovering well
- God made Mary Resilient to endure the possibility of being stoned to death because of her pregnancy supposedly out of wedlock (which wasn't true) (Luke 1: 29-55 NKJV).

Let us make some declarations together:

- I am Resilient
- My family is Resilient
- I shall Recover Well
- My family shall Recover Well
- Because I look to God, I can do all things and I shall not crumble under pressure.

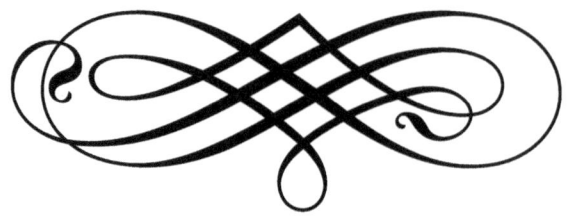

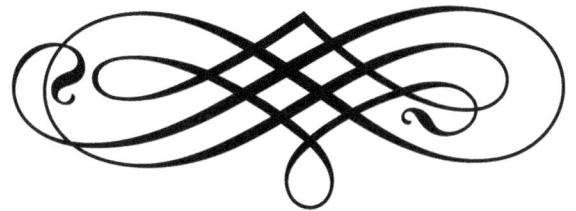

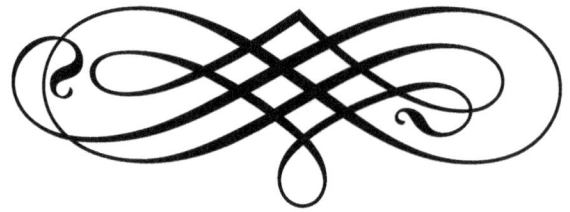

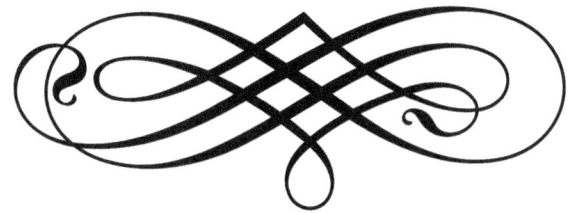

In Ezekiel 3:9 the Berean translates adamant which is said to be harder than flint "Diamond". A Flint was a popular tool used for cutting during the Biblical days

_____
_____
_____
_____
_____
_____
_____
_____
_____
_____
_____
_____
_____
_____
_____
_____
_____
_____
_____
_____
_____
_____
_____

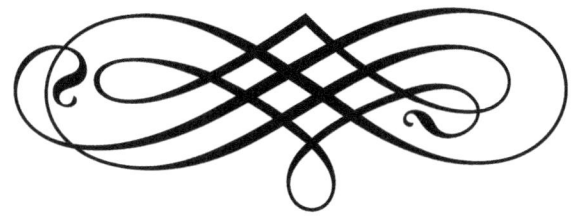

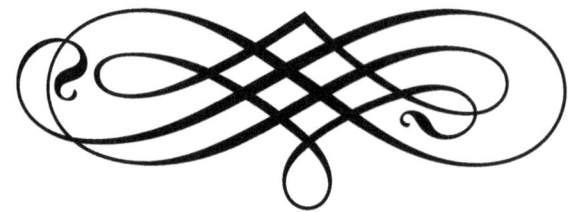

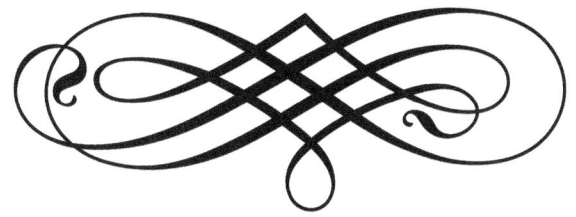

_____

_____

_____

_____

_____

_____

_____

_____

_____

_____

_____

_____

_____

_____

_____

_____

_____

_____

_____

_____

_____

_____

_____

_____

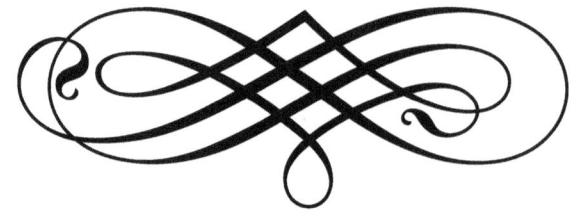

Diamonds are not just ecstatically beautiful....they are dispersers
of Light...a reflection of God's glory

_____

_____

_____

_____

_____

_____

_____

_____

_____

_____

_____

_____

_____

_____

_____

_____

_____

_____

_____

_____

_____

_____

_____

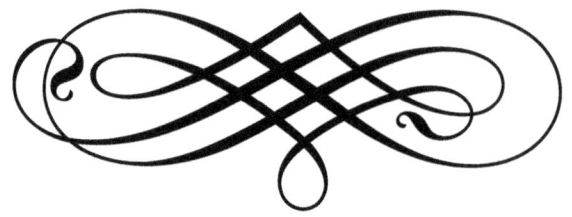

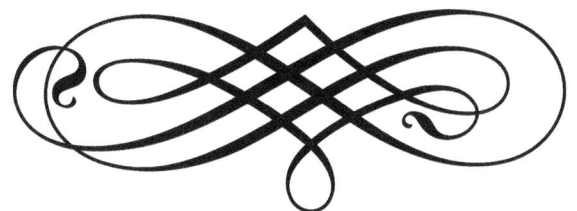

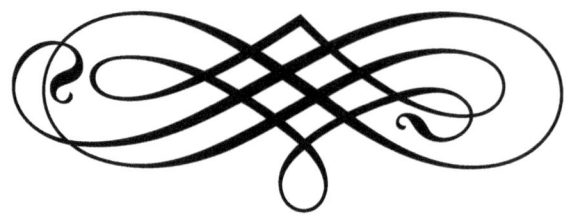

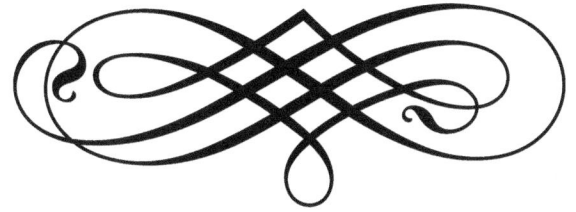

<tab>_____

_____

_____

_____

_____

_____

_____

_____

_____

_____

_____

_____

_____

_____

_____

_____

_____

_____

_____

_____

_____

_____

_____

<tab><tab><tab><tab>31

Diamonds are not just beautiful to the eye...they are tools that help shape some of the toughest of other Diamonds.

_____
_____
_____
_____
_____
_____
_____
_____
_____
_____
_____
_____
_____
_____
_____
_____
_____
_____
_____
_____
_____
_____
_____

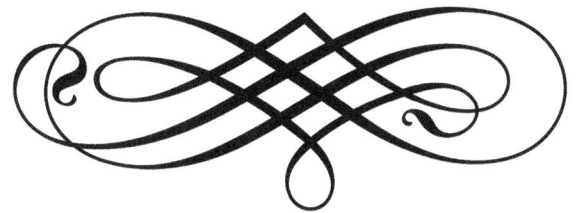

_____

_____

_____

_____

_____

_____

_____

_____

_____

_____

_____

_____

_____

_____

_____

_____

_____

_____

_____

_____

_____

_____

_____

_____

Valuable

Diamonds are very valuable. When obtaining home insurance, most policies give you the option to cover personal items. One of the next questions asked to determine the amount of coverage needed is how much are the Valuables in the home? This is in case there is a burglary or a fire in the home. Then they are broken down into categories; jewelry being one of the ones that is allowed the most coverage. This is because diamonds and gemstones can be very expensive, they are sometimes one of the most Valuable items in most dwellings.

Just like that homeowner, who is willing to pay upward premiums to insure their diamonds are covered and protected. God values you and I (His creation) so much that He sent His only begotten Son to insure that we would not be stolen by the thief or perish in a fiery eternity. We are God's living and breathing Diamonds. Thank you, God, for seeing us as Valuable . For we know He loves us with an everlasting Love (Jeremiah 31:3 NKJV).

Let's have a Cultivating moment.

We just read how Valuable we are to God. What are some of your most Valuable possessions in life and why?
Take this time to regurgitate your reasons and find corresponding scripture if you like.
This will help you begin to cultivate your heart to align value and love what God loves and hate what God hates (Romans 12:9, NKJV)

- _____
- _____
- _____
- _____
- _____
- _____
- _____
- _____
- _____
- _____
- _____
- _____

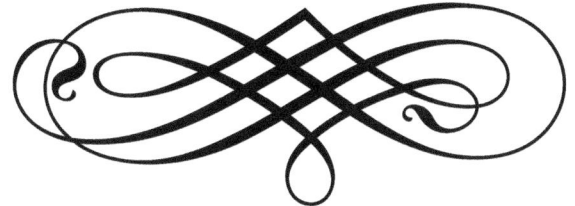

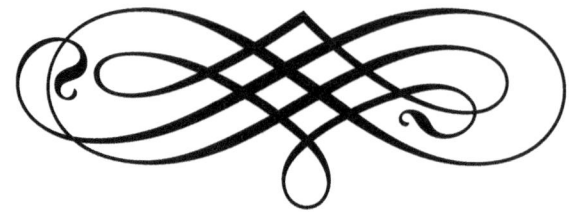

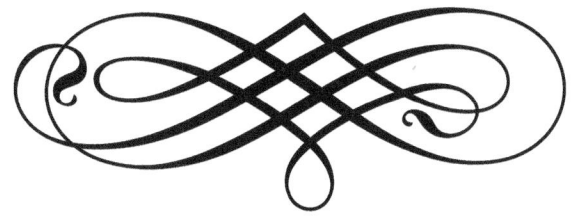

Proverbs 3:15 Says that you are more precious that jewels

_____

_____

_____

_____

_____

_____

_____

_____

_____

_____

_____

_____

_____

_____

_____

_____

_____

_____

_____

_____

_____

_____

_____

_____

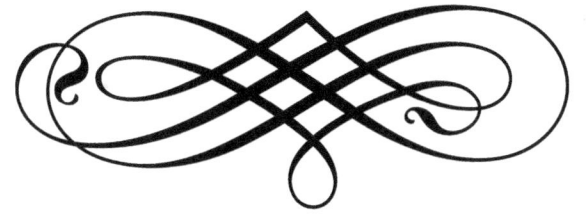

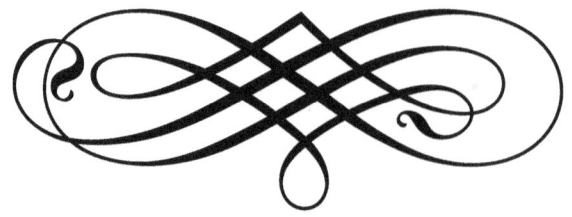

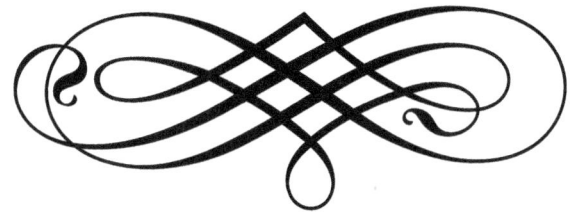

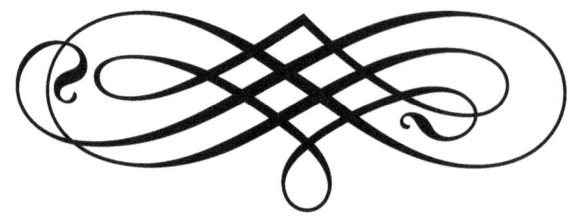

<hr />

<hr />

<hr />

<hr />

<hr />

<hr />

<hr />

<hr />

<hr />

<hr />

<hr />

<hr />

<hr />

<hr />

<hr />

<hr />

<hr />

<hr />

<hr />

<hr />

<hr />

<hr />

<hr />

You are a jewel....a gem... in a Royal diadem

_____
_____
_____
_____
_____
_____
_____
_____
_____
_____
_____
_____
_____
_____
_____
_____
_____
_____
_____
_____
_____
_____
_____
_____
_____
_____

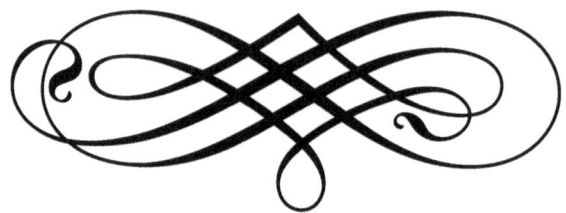

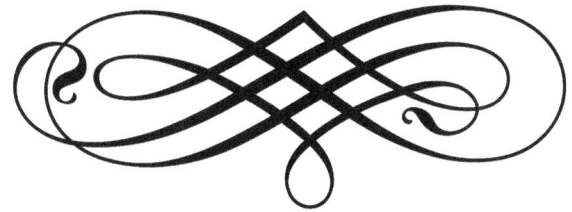

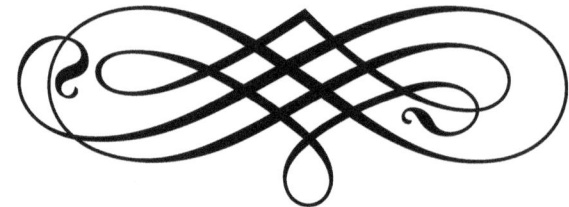

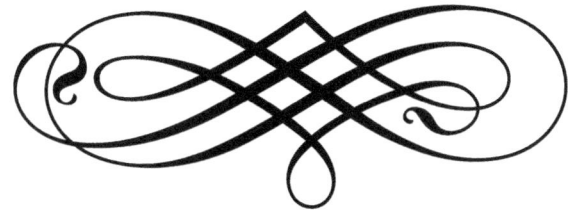

Become...... By Spending time in God's presence....just Become ...Become
God's version of you!

_____
_____
_____
_____
_____
_____
_____
_____
_____
_____
_____
_____
_____
_____
_____
_____
_____
_____
_____
_____
_____
_____
_____
_____
_____
_____
_____
_____
_____
_____
_____

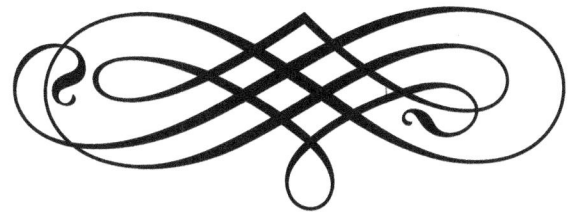

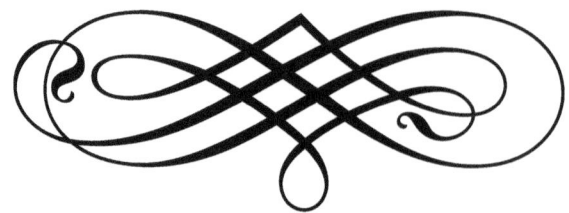

Unique

Every Diamond is unique. No two diamonds are the same. The variety of shapes that diamonds are available to choose from like oval, pear, princess, heart, etc. are an indication of how the gemologist had to navigate the diamonds uniqueness of each one. The shape is the result of their skillful hand having to delicately navigate their delicate inclusions, rough edges and flaws to determine the less destructive way to get the most value out of each individual one. Sounds familiar? We are fearfully and wonderfully made as well. God has given us our own Unique characteristics, personality, fingerprints, gifts talents and abilities.

Let's Celebrate Your Uniqueness.

What physical characteristic did God give to you that is unique? Blue eyes? A heart shaped birth mark perhaps? Use this moment to encourage yourself. You are special! You are Unique! God said VERY GOOD when He finished you (Genesis 1:7 NKJV)

_____

_____

_____

_____

_____

There is an evil going viral. This evil is called COMPARISON. Living in this digital and instantaneous age, anyone in the world can share their digitalized version of themselves through a vast number of filters and augment realities. However, not everyone is aware, and many are deceived. Creating unreachable body image goals predicated on a digitalized version of someone who is unable to achieve the look naturally themselves.

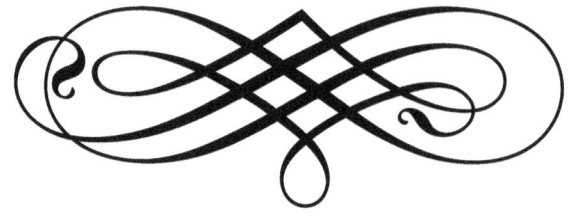

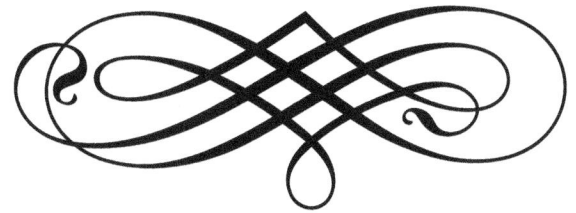

Diamonds are made by pressure. Romans 5: 3-4 says that our own suffering produces endurance and endurance and endurance produces character produces hope....

_____

_____

_____

_____

_____

_____

_____

_____

_____

_____

_____

_____

_____

_____

_____

_____

_____

_____

_____

_____

_____

_____

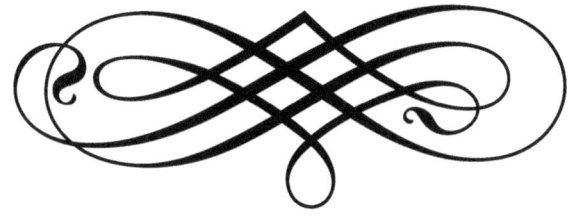

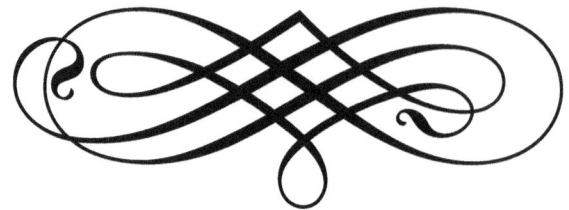

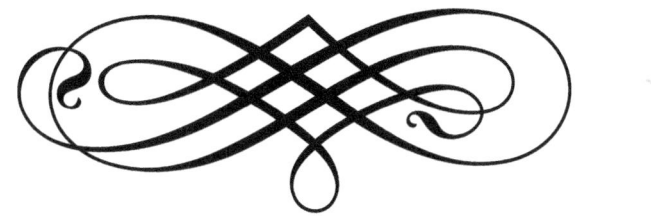

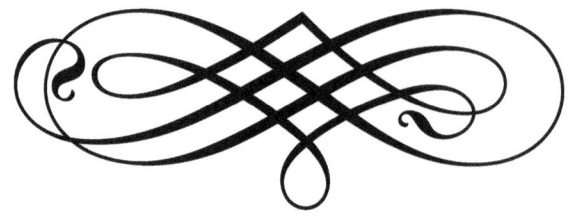

An unknown author said that "Character is who you are when no one is watching" Someone responded back to this unknown author with "But there is always someone watching"

_____

_____

_____

_____

_____

_____

_____

_____

_____

_____

_____

_____

_____

_____

_____

_____

_____

_____

_____

_____

_____

_____

_____

_____

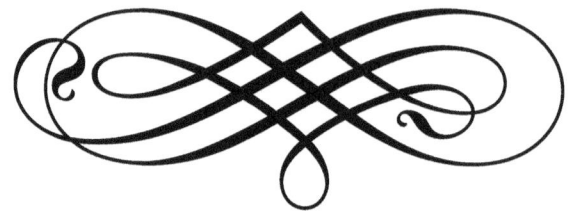

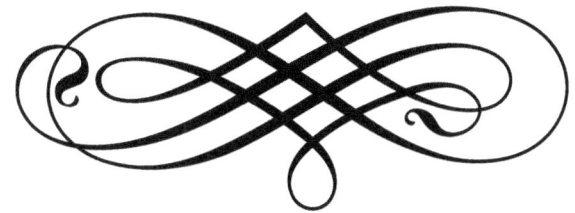

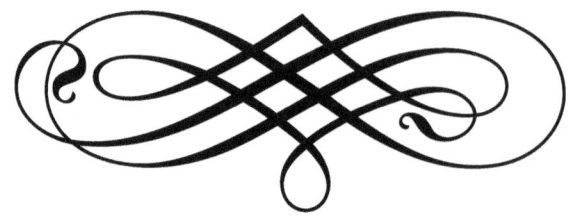

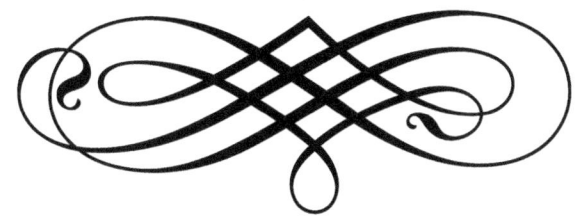

James 1: 2-4 Count it all joy, my brothers, when you meet trials of various kinds, for you know that the testing of your faith produces steadfastness. And let steadfastness have its full effect, that you may be perfect and complete, lacking in nothing

_____

_____

_____

_____

_____

_____

_____

_____

_____

_____

_____

_____

_____

_____

_____

_____

_____

_____

_____

_____

_____

_____

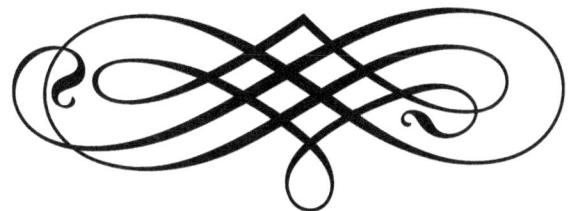

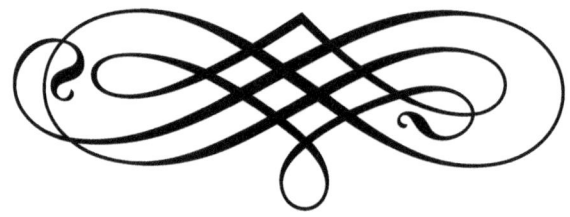

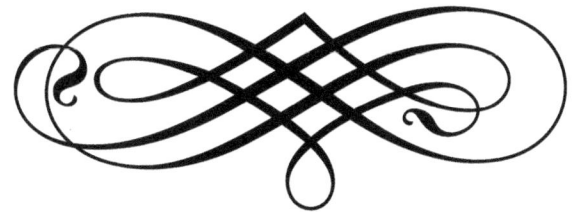

Radiant

Radiant means to send out light. It means to shine or glow brightly. The scripture tells us that Jesus is the Light of the World and He is in You (John 8:12 KJV). Matthew 5:14-16 explains how a City that is on hill cannot hidden and neither how a candle that is lit should be placed under a bushel (NKJV). Just as the purpose of the candle is to give light to the whole house, we are to allow the light of Jesus to shine through our lives. We are to Radiant with God's glory no matter where we go.

Let's have a moment of Reflection.

Do you Radiant with God's glory? Do you allow the light of the Gospel to be seen in and through you? Have you ever heard the expression "You light up a room"? or "There is something about you". Well it's all about perception. It could have been their personality or that person's smile. It also could have been the light of their spirit. Glowing with the glory of God. Allowing the light of Jesus to be seen in and through them like Moses when he returned from being in fellowship with God throughout the book of Exodus chapter 19.

Make a list of how you can allow God's radiance to shine through your life. What are some things that could be dimming your light? It's okay. God loves you. He doesn't condemn us. He lovingly corrects up and strengthens us to be able to do things His way. Because God's ways leads us to life and Godliness. Be sure to write your lists but for now

Let us Pray

Lord, I repent of anything that I may have done that is dimming your light from shining bright in me. Lord, I ask that you forgive me from all unrighteousness and thank you for delivering me from any strongholds that are preventing me from living a life full of your Radiant glory. In Jesus name!

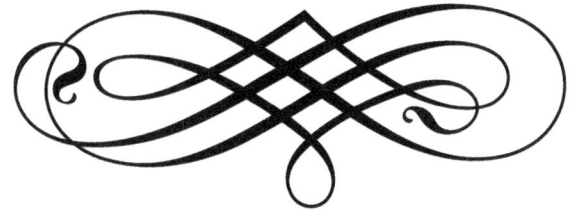

Isaiah 62:3 You shall be a crown of beauty in the hand of the LORD, and a royal diadem in the hand of your God.

_____

_____

_____

_____

_____

_____

_____

_____

_____

_____

_____

_____

_____

_____

_____

_____

_____

_____

_____

_____

_____

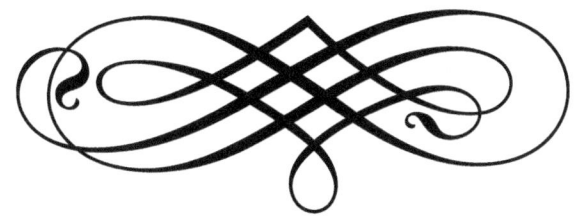

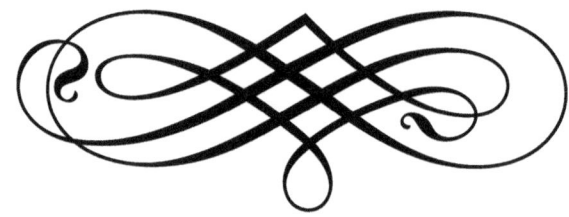

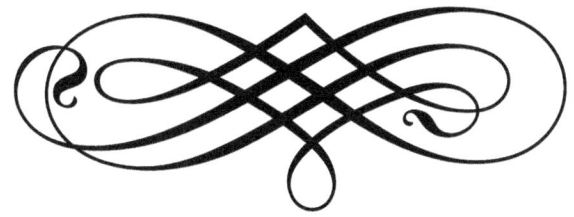

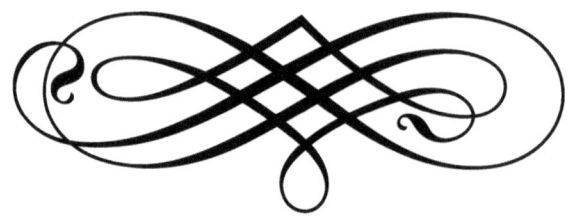

_____

_____

_____

_____

_____

_____

_____

_____

_____

_____

_____

_____

_____

_____

_____

_____

_____

_____

_____

_____

_____

_____

_____

_____

Scintillation: the process of state of emitting flashes or sparkles of light.
Be sure to Scintillate today.

_____

_____

_____

_____

_____

_____

_____

_____

_____

_____

_____

_____

_____

_____

_____

_____

_____

_____

_____

_____

_____

_____

_____

_____

_____

_____

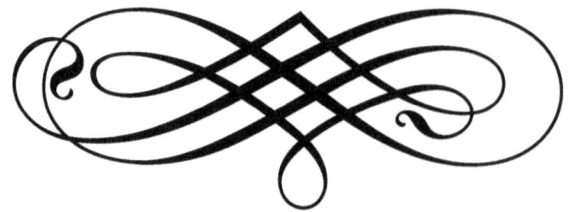

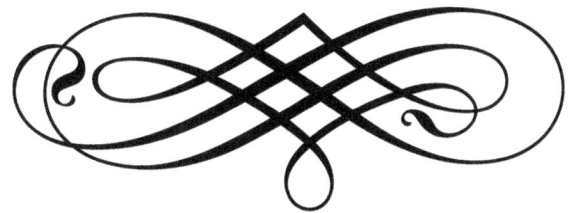

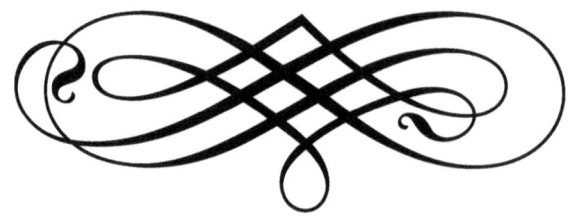

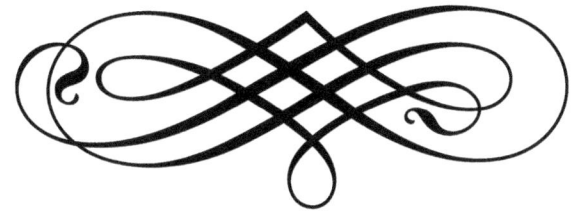

Shine! God's Diamond Shine! Allow the light of God to shine through you

_____

_____

_____

_____

_____

_____

_____

_____

_____

_____

_____

_____

_____

_____

_____

_____

_____

_____

_____

_____

_____

_____

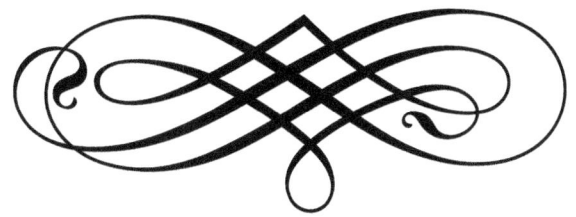

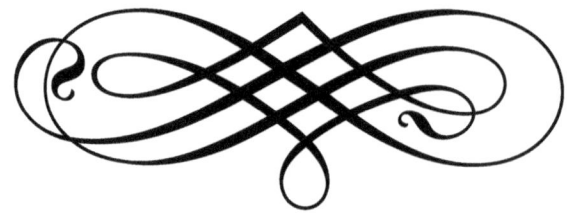

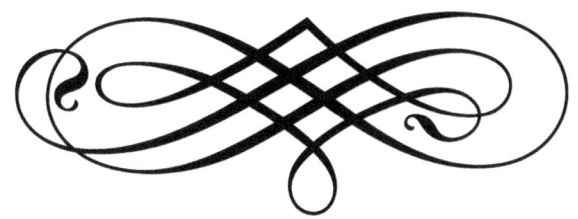

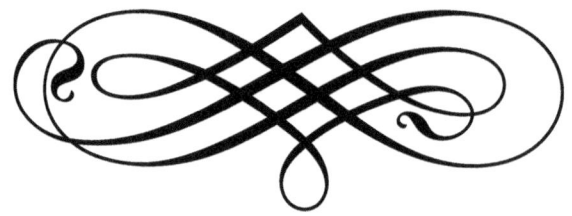

Scintillate

Scintillate means to emit flashes of light while in motion. Scintillation is the process that objects such as diamonds displays visible light or emits ultraviolet light as the result of a high energy source. We recognize this as the flashes or twinkles of light that a diamond ring gives off while being admired on someone's hand.

I particularly love what the process of scintillation represents because when a living and breathing diamond scintillates (You and I); It means that they are not lying dormant in life.

Let's have a moment of Reflection.

In the scriptures, there were many who emitted the light of God and scintillated the character of God. Ester shined as she risked her life to save her people (Ester 5:7, NKJV). Jael scintillated when she sprang into action to subdue Sisera after serving him warm milk and laying a blanket over him to aide him to sleep (Judges 4:19-21 NKJV). David reflected the light of God's glory when He spared King Saul his life while he lay asleep (1 Samuel 24: 3-11 NKJV). In all instances there were choices to be made. Everyday life presents to us choices. It is up to us whether we dim God's light or allow Him to shine through us. All while being certain to pointing all on-lookers back to God's glory. Can you identify an area either in your personal life at home or on the job that God wants to be seen through you? These challenges are many times uncomfortable to our flesh.

Let us Pray

Jesus, you died that we may live. Now you may live through those that believe in your death, burial and resurrection. Forgive me Lord if I have allowed the trials of life to harden my heart and dim my light.

Psalm 27: 1 The Lord is my light and my salvation – Whom shall I fear (Amplified)

_____

_____

_____

_____

_____

_____

_____

_____

_____

_____

_____

_____

_____

_____

_____

_____

_____

_____

_____

_____

_____

_____

_____

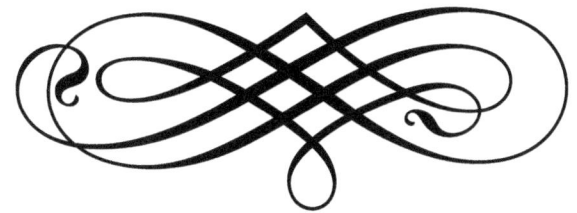

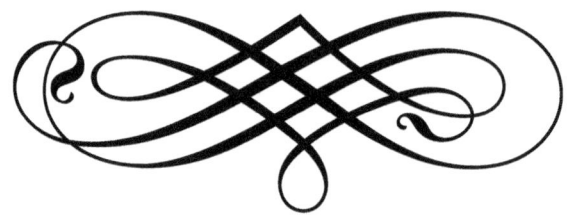

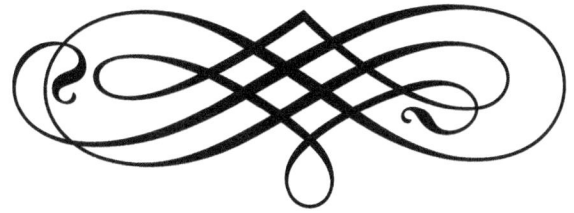

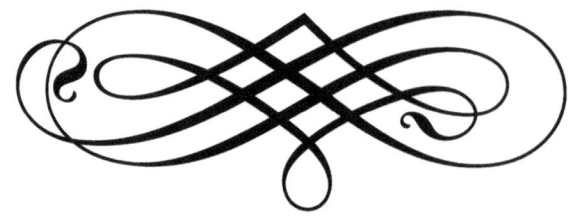

Isaiah 60:1 Arise [from spiritual depression to a new life], shine [be radiant with the glory and brilliance of the LORD]; for your light has come, And the glory and brilliance of the LORD has risen upon you.

_____
_____
_____
_____
_____
_____
_____
_____
_____
_____
_____
_____
_____
_____
_____
_____
_____
_____
_____
_____
_____
_____
_____

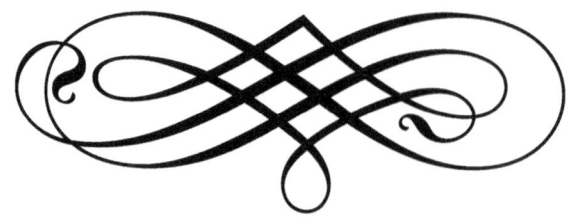

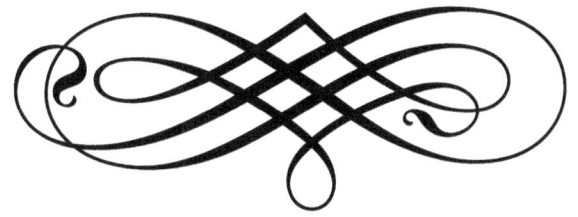

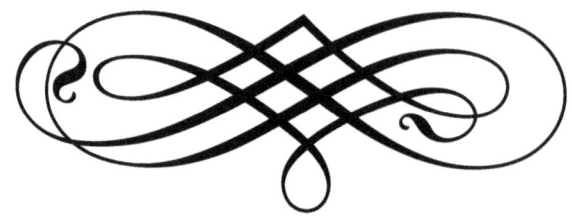

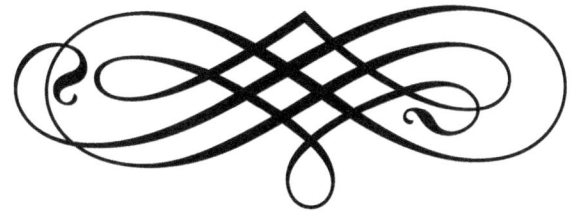

Habakkuk 3:4 His brilliance is like light; rays are flashing from His hand.
This is where His power is hidden.

_____
_____
_____
_____
_____
_____
_____
_____
_____
_____
_____
_____
_____
_____
_____
_____
_____
_____
_____
_____
_____
_____

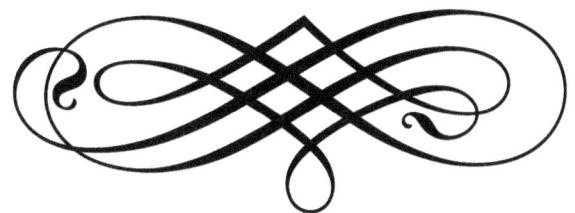

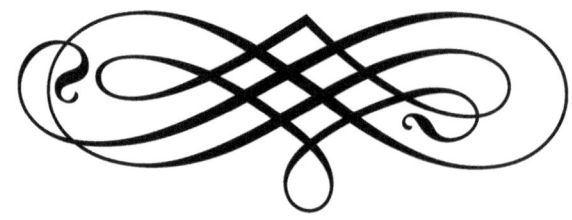

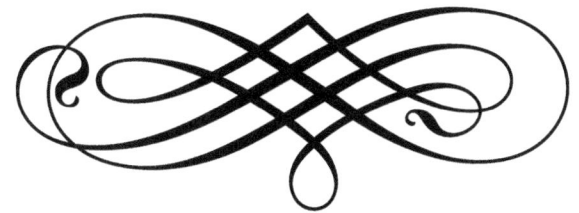

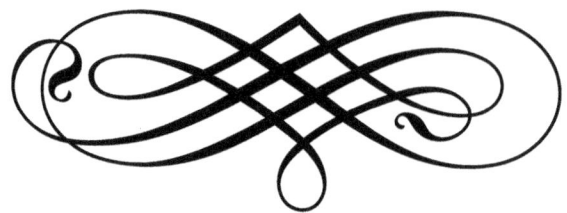

Luke 9:29 As He was praying, the appearance of His face became different [actually transformed], and His clothing became whi te and flashing with the brilliance of lightning. (Amplified)

_____

_____

_____

_____

_____

_____

_____

_____

_____

_____

_____

_____

_____

_____

_____

_____

_____

_____

_____

_____

_____

_____

_____

_____

_____

Treasure

A Treasure is something valuable and meaningful. 2 Corinthians 4:7 says, "But we have this treasure in earthen vessel, that the excellency of power may be of God and not of us (KJV)." This scripture again gives us more evidence that Diamonds which are also treasures are a representation of another's light. These treasures reflects God's glory and does not take glory of its own! Holy Spirit is our treasure, and we are the earthen vessel if you allow. He shines through us. He gives us hope and solace as we yield to give Him glory.

Let's have a moment of Reflection.

What do you treasure in your life? Would others be able to peer into your life and immediately be able to identify what your treasure is? The answer is yes. Unfortunately, the thing that we treasure or value the most isn't always something we are proud of or good for us. However, whether positive or negative, there is always evidence of its presence in our lives. Treasures tend to leave Hansel and Gretel crumbs (from the fairy tale story) in our lives. For example: those who treasure sports, would likely have their favorite sports team apparel or sports memorabilia displayed throughout their living space. Likely frequenting quite amount of their games.

Diamonds are treasures, and most owners take exquisite care of them. However, I want to remind you, that you are God's living and breathing Diamond. You are His prize treasure, and He wants you to allow Him to take extra care of you as well. This can only be accomplished when you surrender. God is our Creator, but He also wants to be our Father. He is also a gentleman; He leaves the choice to receive Him as Savior and Lord up to us (mankind). Will you make a decision for Christ today? The Bible says if you do the following you SHALL be saved.

Repent of your sins, receive His Son (Jesus) as Lord and Savior and believe that Jesus was crucified, died, was buried, and rose again for the sins of man. You shall be saved and thy house (Romans 10:9&10 NKJV).

Let us Pray

Jesus, I come before you Lord repenting of all of my sins. Come into my heart, change me, Lord. I don't want to live this way any longer, but I cannot do this on my own. I need you Jesus to wash me, cleanse me from all unrighteousness. I hear people say that I am your treasure now I want to know that I am your treasure. In Jesus name (Romans 10:9 &10).

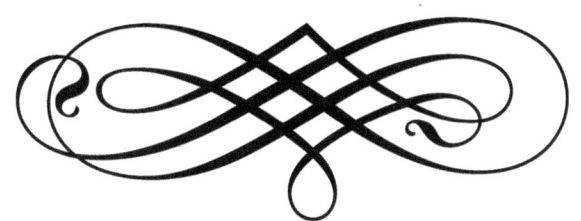

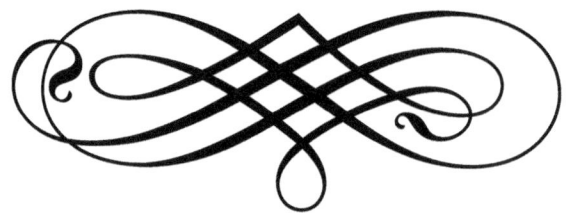

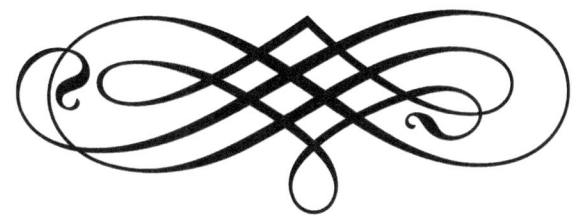

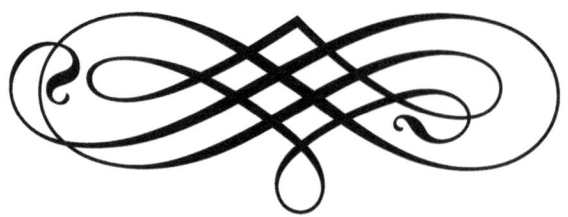